TRIO POETRY
1

TRIO POETRY
1

Will Colhoun
Robert Johnstone
David Park

Blackstaff Press

© Will Colhoun, Robert Johnstone, David Park, 1980.

Published by Blackstaff Press Limited, 3 Galway Park, Dundonald, Belfast, BT16 0AN, with the assistance of the Arts Council of Northern Ireland.

All rights reserved. No part of this publication may be reproduced, stored in a retrieval system, or transmitted, in any form or by any means, electronic, mechanical, photocopying, recording or otherwise, without the prior permission of Blackstaff Press Limited.

Conditions of Sale: This book shall not without the written consent of the Publishers first given be lent, re-sold, hired out or otherwise disposed of by way of trade in any form of binding or cover other than that in which it is published.

ISBN 0 85640 164 1

Printed in Northern Ireland by Belfast Litho Printers Limited.

Contents

Will Colhoun

The Mind's Not an Unbarred Grating	3
A Kind of Reality Intrudes	4
A Vain Attempt	5
We See Through a Glass Darkly	6
Reaction to a Review	7
Emotion Recollected in Tranquillity	8
To Meet the Faces that I Meet	9
Do It Yourself	10
Brotherly Love	11
Love's Labour	12
Something Hardens in a Man's Soul	13
Fools Rush In	14
Spiderman	15
Still Life	16
Only a Thin and Conscious Layer	17
Final Statement	18
Blowing the Gaff	19

Robert Johnstone

In Time of Peace	23
As If It Never Happened	25
Adelaide	26
Scientific Fiction	27
The Postman's Bedtime Story	28
Divorce	29
There Existed Another Ending to the Story of O	31
Autobiography	32
Before Sleep	33
What We Did on Our Holidays	35
Working with Cauliflowers	36

Every Cache 37
New Incidents in the Life of Shelley 41

David Park
Lame Duck 47
The Piano Miracle 48
Snow-drift 49
The Fire at Crymble's Music Shop 50
Beautiful Lofty Things 52
Boys' Game 53
Threading the Stars 54
Walking Over the Troubles 55
My Grandfather 56
Pat Jennings 57
The Things that Frighten 58
At the Vincent Van Gogh Museum 60
The Stained Shroud 61
Anne Frank's Shroud 62
The Climber in the Cherry Blossom Tree 63
Teaching Billy to Read 64
Violence 65

WILL COLHOUN

The Mind's Not an Unbarred Grating

Once swishing up wetted coal dust,
A polished nugget plopped down the unbarred grating.
Stooping and scoop-diggering confident fingers
I prised out, dwarfed-pig-like, a drowned mouse,
Rubbery hairless with china-fine curled feet.
The electric shock of it jolting my elbow
I screeched it free, then shuddered away.

On the tip of my brain an analogy teeters
And for some days now has refused to spill.
The mind's not an unbarred grating
To be entered with consummate skill.

A Kind of Reality Intrudes

In formaldehyde in jars the snakes coiled staringly.

As first-formers we played a simple chicken game,
Slithering the heavy jars to the edge of the stone sill,
Leaving them precariously teetering while Sir droned on.

The excitement of the jungle was in the classroom
Without the sweat, the tangled growth, mosquito bites.
Vicarious experience became an opiate, later induced
By TV dosage in our sitting rooms.

Until one day a jar powdered splashingly
And oiled snake elasticated across the stone floor.
What riot terror then! I remember screaming.

Life made more real, not living dreaming.

A Vain Attempt

Is it that I saw you typewriter
As some kind of status symbol
To be ostentatiously placed,
The light of my ego's eye?
For, since that monetary commitment
I have avoided too close contact,
Sidestepped your cryptic stare
And sought out gentler foes.

Typing this is a vain attempt
To stop you glaring discontent.

We See Through a Glass Darkly

On the steps of Manchester Art Gallery
The orderly framed vision was blurred
Then flicked from consciousness by a seeming harder reality.

Pushing ridiculous furniture in a battered pram,
Her Munch face splintered by tears,
A woman trailed past three descending children.

A grey wind made nonsense of her thin dress
And I followed, voyeurism struggling with concern
While oncoming shoppers tore glued stares and fled.

An older overcoated man caught up
And recrimination began, the big-eyed children
Completing composition, adding poignancy to the whole.

Then furious walking, gesticulation, gasping tears.
I'll give her my jacket! No more objective sociology,
This time I'll step inside the frame.

The row becalmed, she raised a shawl.
Had she managed to fool us all?

Reaction to a Review

The pejorative '…clutching their slim volumes…'
    has nettled me
Weighing, as I am, my own vulnerable collection.

That word 'slim' has caused the pain.
Yield is important, supply must be maintained,

While already I can feel resources somewhat drained.

Emotion Recollected in Tranquillity

The squat moon-rocket grain feeders
Were hauled and twisted each morning
And leggy hens jerked quickly to the meal.
Then dipping heads, a tinny pecking,
A Goon Show chorus of contentment.

Once, stooping, lifting and twisting,
A bloated rat, bean-bag heavy,
Tumbled on my boot and crawl-scuttled away.
The searing: *It could have fallen down inside,*
Curled tight my toes paralysing movement.

Then hardened Joe caught up and kicked,
Rugby-ball skying and thudding the rat
Within inches of my terror, where underbelly
And needle teeth exposed my dread.

I roared and ran, fear gnawing through my head.

To Meet the Faces that I Meet

I have this mask I present to faces
When I know they are spotlighting mine.
It served me well at da's funeral
Conveyed the role to perfection that time.

Yet it melted the morning that tears fell
And I fled from them all to a room
Where my sister administered whiskey
And I coughed out my grief, until soon,
Like the audience applauding their clapping
My crying achieved like refrain...

I assembled my mask like a trouper,
Plunged into the role once again.

Do It Yourself

You never let me saw
I only held the wood.
Despite the murderous thoughts
I helped you all I could.

'A chip off the old block,'
Barmen and friends would say.
The chip I shouldered grew
And would not fall away.

I felt myself excluded
Used mainly to impress
Always kept outside you,
A kind of formal dress.

At least that's how I viewed it
So one day resentment's elf
Prompted me to stab you with
The barbed, 'Do it yourself!'

Brotherly Love

When nine, I grudge-tugged Robin and David to the pictures,
Their four and five an eldest brother's heartache.
Firm father-like I spent the conciliatory thruppence
On penny gob-stoppers, a good half-film suck.

Once inside that velvety Aladdin's cave
I relished in the generosity of Sultanship
And forgave their tell-tale pact against me,
Assuaged by the eminence of my role.

Then David (it would be him) cough-shot his sweet
And it stickily rolled, shattering content.
Bugger responsibility! It ached you every time.
I thumped him hard, then quickly gave him mine.

Love's Labour

I was chauvinist drunk when my twins were born.
Hours later a wide-eyed triumphant wife,
Led me to the most beautiful moment of my life.
They lay beached creatures in separate glass tanks.
Then Laura moved an arm, Glenda turned her head
And there was an ache of love and a blurring
And a reaching but no contact, no caressing.

I hope I have those feelings again
And there's no partition to swell the pain.

Something Hardens in a Man's Soul

'But I never opened my mouth!'

Recognizing the exaggerated outrage,
I oiled the troubled waves with:
'I never said you did.'

'Then I'm not moving, I'm staying here!'
Swivelled heads probing for the signs of fear.

He has to be hit, it's the only way.
Move slowly and let the anger work.
The watchers demand their pound of flesh.
It's you or him or they eat you up.

Smack! Throb-flush his cheek, red alert in his eyes,
He must not retaliate, a move and he dies.

Silence glares in the room, shakings subside,
Eyes lock unto books, while, alone on my side,
I lick wounds of victory which hardness will heal!;
At what cost to my principles, my pride in my zeal?

Fools Rush In

Fuelling then stirring the discussion
I ladle out 'Kissing Families'
Then season with a dash of wisdom:
'We must experience love to be able to show it.'

Leaning back to savour the reaction
I am alarmed by sniffled sobs
From Heather (father left) and regret again
A lack of tact comparable to that wincing time
When forcing gaiety, I teased Margaret,
(A likeable, ebullient and spina bifida child) with:
'I hope they don't turn out like you.'

I meant my twins and her ebulliency,
Yet how to say this when her face registered.
I prattled on, making flushed replies
To wipe out with talk the dark pain in her eyes.

Spiderman

As a notorious junior he had eaten spiders, drunk ink
And now, nicknamed, labelled by all
He played the part outrageously;
Could fart to order or trip fantastically,
Size thirteens providing the perfect alibi.

Banned from maths, I can't remember why,
He came to me, sat at the back.
Our ways the same one afternoon
I caught him up and attempted to forge
An early pact to counter future skirmishing.

It worked, and he began the tales
Of fishing, shooting, snaring, in a world
He graced with ease and certainty.
Once in his pigeon-loft he rhymed off
Numbered leg-rings of randomly chosen birds.

He left, to butcher pigs in a local factory.
Recently I was chokingly told how:
'…through boot and all…' he'd axed his foot.

There you go! It's tumbling time again Spiderman.
Don't do it for applause — ignore them if you can.

Still Life

When the bomb thundered in Belfast
People seemed locked in mid-stride
Flinks of metal twinkled high
And somewhere a baby cried.

Then like a snapshot granted life
There was movement and purpose once more.
People strode on their way and a curious few
Rushed to gawk at the city's new sore.

Only a Thin and Conscious Layer

The crushing thoughts keep stumbling in
Then it's wincing time once more.
Names tell if Protestant or Catholic dead,
As if that mattered, life is the cardinal core.

It's not fellow-feeling deeply felt
That keeps prejudice from bursting out,
But only a thin and conscious layer
Permeable, wind-blown, subject to doubt.

Final Statement

My thought is a northern flinty kind
Where reason thrives and soft words die.
I find no peace in peaty sentiment,
No resting place in a past's sad cry.

Blowing the Gaff

I long to experience myself in print,
To create a stir through the written word,
To be interviewed by Robinson and Bragg,
Then shatter the illusion, show it's absurd.

Van Gogh's an exception that proves the rule,
The garret is warmed by ambition's flame,
It's all a con, you can take my tip,
This quest for art's just an ego trip.

ROBERT JOHNSTONE

In Time of Peace

Like true levellers
we assumed a high place
to issue manifestoes
to overlook the populated plain
to delight in such ironies.

At campfires in hideouts
irregulars with their fashionable
asthma and camouflage
would invite us as brothers
to share their liberated food.

The lady of the demesne
offered the loan of her stables
with a large grant.
We weren't seduced by her applause
or their supplies.

Like time travellers
on top of that peak
that grew nearer the sky
we devised the future
as we logged the lower struggle

picturing Eden
as a local valley,
finding a lesson in the fact
that Christ died on an eminence.
Raised above attack

by renouncing the stealable
everything was a small price
for peace of mind,
security, salvation.
But even when left to our own devices,

perfection and the growth of food,
the sore, the weed of doubt sprang.
Were we cultivating
the drama of our souls,
less modest than Adamites?

Was it moral to observe
armies war beneath us,
each man aware what determined
general inhumanities,
each assuming private luck?

That was the common sense
we'd got sick of
but found waiting for us
when all else failed or
failed to fail, as

the acceptable height of war became
a level of acceptable peace.
Living like this we look back
to our dreams of the future
and earn reward.

Our mascot was a spider
that saw with strange eyes
and danced in suspense
unawares on a beautiful
naive pattern.

Now I keep thinking
that this was a killing floor
that our
beautiful obsession proved
useless if correct.

As If It Never Happened

This could be the ninth time.
I turn the lock imagining
a booby trap.

You feel nothing. When it explodes,
time stops, I switch
to another identical life.

In one world, relatives,
lovers mourn. But already
I am in the next and the door opens easily

as it always does and I sit at the wheel
and switch on, feeling only a quick pulse
and the strangeness of it all.

My self disintegrating.
My self partly integrating
with the air.

Adelaide

The Brits are making a lot
of noise in that damn chopper,
hanging their narrow searchlight
in garish equilibrium
to scan the ghetto for sin.
When they go away again
a proof's still ranged before me,
a carpet of lights from here
to the hills, one each for all
who thought to choose the same life.

I stand with my back against
the writing on the wall, feeling
not safe, but at home at least.
Out there starts Comanche land
with a different class of
graffito, but at night and
distance I'm unable to
discriminate between shade
and nuance. No. Surrendered
to N.I. Rail because I'm
flirting with routine, I've got
nothing to do but wait and
play inside my head with words
for their unnecessary
music.

Scientific Fiction

In the Scientific Shoe Company
a box for X-rays of the feet
of course.

It's dark at four, the shop's glowing,
my feet have frozen near the bone
as I kill time before a movie
set in a decadent future,
feeling a relic of love made,
a memory of Eden,
where I believed in Adam's dream
at the drop of your pants
and all I got was knowledge.

If I woke and found it true
I'd want things as they are now
but us reborn inside:
I'd kill time in a new Gomorrah
gorged with love,
like Clark Kent
my super-vision would detect
cosmonettes who mine the moon.
I'd be warm and happy
in my Scientific shoes.

The Postman's Bedtime Story

Pavements erupt where roots creep
the length of the avenue
underneath our static homes

dismantling the life we built
to accidental beauty,
disinterested of course in

our aesthetic: tonight I
share a function of the trees,
to utter without understanding.

Lost, you've turned your back on me
to fall asleep intact and
thinking of the door between.

Think instead of my hand (which
even now creeps under you)
as a root, disinterested

in your aesthetic, turning
you, if only you'd lie still,
to accidental beauty.

Divorce

Sorting her effects I found
a drama book which had
a photo with this caption:
'Each began, in his own way,
to destroy cardboard boxes.'

Apparently political,
the actors learning rules,
painfully, their abstract games
valid since nonverbal: he
says they broke homes, ideals.

Our politics rejected
pain, or the principle of pain.
We spoke without God, seriously
of black and white as shades of grey,
not continuous. Now we've

broken the house quakes, I push
my nose between cracks or crack
jokes sublimely, pretending
it was immaterial,
cardboard certain as concrete.

We could only have been certain
that some cupboard or corner
would remain unfamiliar.
Still she lists everything: between
lines, what's she not saying?

Down crackly phones she says
she knows that words like 'home'
depend on where the heart is,
that what goes on around 'love'
is what makes the difference.

If we don't touch, we can't speak.
She won't know how, standing
where we lived, with all our
clutter now packed in boxes,
half truths, our cheap china, break.

I was only ever half
serious, each new quotation
another ornament. I look
now for some effect, some event
that we forgot we shared.

There Existed Another Ending to the Story of O

'*Not death, but a new setting, waits for us*'
Joseph Brodsky, 'The Candlestick'

I can accept that someone understands
your transparent life in a foreign place,
that he plays your body like an instrument,
that your scent stays on his clothes all day.

He likes to look at you put on your shoes,
he tells you what underwear he wants you to buy,
he watches from the bed as you move
across the room in long sunlight (for we

each agree it's always like autumn there). His
car's parked under the trees. He finds leaves caught
for months behind the bumpers. It's something loose
you fear at the edges of your day, so

on your own you check windows, the glass door
— there's only windows and air between us —
but something indulges a fetish,
occupies gaps when you're gone; for instance,

the miracle of radio, which I
accept, Chopin performed in your empty flat,
polkas that greet your return, for scenes of our
mad love control us, they don't belong.

Can somebody be learning things are
independent? Why else am I returned
to that October in my dream of blood?
Why else would you tremble now, recalling

how I broke glass and wished it was your bones?
But here are your perfumed clothes which wait
innocently still where you left them. See?
Always, really, nothing's been disturbed.

Autobiography

To find ourselves, but with everything between our ears
however we try still on our own terms,
we lie in a silent room wearing stereo headphones,
for all we want's Mozart and the illusion of a centre.

We took our flatmate Faith
for granted until she
scrawled a thin green line on paper
and called it her Self Portrait.

How should we have acted?
How do you suppose a body could act
towards a business relation
birdsong made spastic?

Nurses forced her room, she squatting,
face plastered with poster paint,
among messages she'd scribbled on the wall
like warnings from the ghetto of a future city.

Our friends have found you out.
They were here, they are gone.
Our face became sore with grinning.
We wash for bed imagining

the girl in hospital sedated dreams
sunlit water nurses carry her in bowls
another form of air,
the element she'll live in next.

Suds mollify our cheeks as we remove mascara
but you still catch flecks of red about the nose.
The mirror face is ours once.
Now you will lie between these sheets where I put a knife

and think of that man in the bank today.
Deaf mute, embarrassing, he waved his arms at the glass
but failed to be understood.
The only sound he made was the creaking of his boots.

Before Sleep
(after 'Coleccion Nocturna' by Pablo Neruda)

Yawns and coffee sludge clog extremities
waiting for the midnight flight.

If I stuck it here long enough
I'd meet the whole world moping round
awaiting my important visitor,
each in turn of interest
to that president of that unexplored plateau
who obliges you to carry her official bags
which are too heavy.

The details hardly vary:
footsteps like a kiss, kiss like footsteps,
she's hot from a conference on Nothing,
carries bald communiqués of blank paper,
always packs dossiers on all my friends,
always deceiving.

I can see me now, driving back
through unfamiliar streets in the dark scary districts,
glimpsing them on corners, rubbing shoulders on a terrace
where we cheer in tens of thousands
me at centre forward.

Those fully qualified in history and fear
can't help admitting I'm a second Best.

But,
and here I use a metaphor,
the ref gives a penalty, I dissent, am sent off,
the ghosts of my heroic moves meet me along the tunnel.

I'm about to go through it all again
for the black jumbo's booming like sea.

Before I have to leave
let me suggest that, in this room,
after we've disappeared,
there'll be something of each of us,
not much, something indefinite
left floating.

For that reason I try to ignore timetables
and concentrate on air instead,
on various points in the sky
or an immobile face in the arrivals lounge,
aware a part of everything's
ready to become part of me.

I name each landmark by such star gazing.

On clear nights at least.

What We Did on Our Holidays

That oil in plastic bottles,
lighter than sea water, couldn't sink.
I dropped one to prove it — so:
it bobbed up impossibly.

I stepped from the ladder, easy
now, knowing my awkwardness,
wedged myself between petrol,
reciprocating rubber.

The Seagull wobbled us to where
we'd moored to a regatta buoy
among a thousand yachts
from Panama, England, U.S.

Like their steel cables a conger
hung dead in the still tide.
That was the night I read them
'Riding Westward': they thought me odd.

— As Boat Clubs found our poverty
eccentric. Out of water
in Millisle, Port Oriel, Howth, Rosslare...
though pretty girls seemed prettier.

Often we were lead astray
(by Shannon Air Radio)
and typically we hit a shark
basking in a shoal of mackerel.

But I still hear the Mercury
echoing as we skimmed
in an arcade of our own noise,
a tunnel of love we paid

to get into, a time skein, with
Ireland on our right hand, the sun
over Clear, and nothing to the south
but trouble between us and Spain.

Working with Cauliflowers

I dress them for the stand by exposing their hearts.
The shop knife makes clean, quick cuts,
I snap their big leaves at the pale stalks.
I hold one to consider its weight

and see fields of rows of cauliflowers,
whose brainy hearts lie true as eyeballs
beneath vacant blue. They've hermetic purpose,
are swollen with contemplation.

Equally crucial are these
hard foam gobbets banked up
where people surge and ebb about them.
The sun is describing its arc over

white forests, self absorbed till now, that tumble
when a woman rummages in my display,
wary of buying the last live thing, a caterpillar
in a soft litter of eggs and dung.

A mere worker in the Food Industry,
Made-to-Measure Department, I sell her one
in an example too big for the paper.
She takes it away awkwardly under her arm.

Every Cache

1
Every cache, the deed box, plastic wallets,
a leather pouch, even a nylon sock,
and all the pockets where we'd find a roll
of grubby notes are emptied now. The affairs
you mystified with such peasant cunning
against another war or invasion
from the South have been tidied up into
sensible investments. You'd be surprised
to see yourself from here or at how much
of what you did for us is left — forty
years of love in one ailing memory
that's never opened, and all my childhood,
attitudes of yours that will become mine.

2
Eight foot tall
or the shape of Santa Claus
or you sit in your chair
as if it were made for you
to sleep after minutes reading.
Your arms drop
gradually crumpling the paper.
I don't think you ever read a *Telegraph* right through.

You're up before us on a summer morning,
vapour lies across the empty lots,
dust has gathered in the gutters,
a finer dust will settle on your shoes,

or again it's winter and inside the cab
feels colder than outside
and your breath clings to the windscreen
and the van sounds like you, bronchitic,

the old Ford with eight horses
under that gullwing bonnet
or the Austin with column change
and oil and ignition lights like stars.

3
He's a high clear forehead
a debonair moustache
a thornproof jacket
a cardigan that slopes over his belly.

Solidly my father
stands eating a plum
head cocked like a critic
and strikes bargains quickly
with the man in the pork pie hat
who carries a clipboard and agrees
about the quality of goods
under a wall of crates thirty foot high
that's oranges from Haifa
or apples off the freezer trucks
packed in an orchard in France.

Meanwhile I play along a library of palettes.

At the corner of a Cypriot box I see a rotten fruit
a cushion like a tennis ball of blue blancmange.

There are lemons wrapped in medicated tissues
that have gold pictures of the Venus de Milo.

There are bunches of grapes in barrels full of cork
and you pluck them out like presents from a lucky dip.

There are melons in woodwool like a tray of ostrich eggs
and each callipygous peach has her own safe bed.

The lorries nudge in with inches to spare
among narrow lanes of produce.
All are just painted red
the merchant's name
three dimensional.
On the grille of one's
a sprig of white heather
through a polished hubcap
off an American car.

My father deals with the Catholics too.
They've taken their name from their vans
to avoid embarrassment.

I stand in the wooden office
between the spiral stair
and the warm smelling one-bar fire
and my father takes up so much room
as Ambrose asks me how old I am
before he gives me a carton of mushrooms
shaped like the studs in my father's shirts.

A man in an oilskin apron
stirs a bath full of herring
with a pole encrusted in years of scales.
He takes us to the current sight
a steely bearded cod
whose tail lollops outside the metal tray.

My father slips past in his low smooth car.
It has chrome strips, extra spotlamps and leather upholstery

4
Various instants I'm not with you,
waiting at the Heysham boat
before you saw I'd come,
leaning over a fence at the crossroads
of an August evening,
were you thinking of that job you didn't take
in Chicago forty years ago,
or the trawlers parked like dodgems
on our pilgrimage to Aberdeen?

Times you thought I wasn't there
and the sight of you surprised me
I should have used the word 'love'
and didn't.

Opportunities we miss,
moments of each other's lives
we only imagine
help to define us.

But the wonder you took care to teach
for every thing you worked with
was innocent and true.
Like that
we flourish, as we're born to do.

New Incidents in the Life of Shelley

I

After he drowned he appeared to us
riding an incendiary balloon,
all flame, fidgeting with odd gestures.

He settled like a leaf on a lawn,
his craft consumed itself and floated
up as ash. Stumbling forward he frowned

as if at the effort, then steadied
and opened these ghastly eyes, quite void
but also clearly disappointed

to have landed here. He sounded loud
or nervy, and though he shared our qualms
for the present, we loved what he said.

His words burst like particles of charm,
he seemed to give everything new names.

II

Not from our dreams, not from our daft cadres
but from somewhere real, the free enclave we
know inside but can't annex, static or

messages are picked up from the tiny
pirate, Radio Shelley. He reads our odes
over the air, sends reports from countries

claiming to be still at peace, where crops grow
and only the facts are changed to protect
our innocence. At his dangerous modes

of thought valves buzz and blush in our old set
on the cleared tea table. Just to have heard
his programme and talk too loud about it

can cost promotion, yet we grab each word.
We demand contact with that better world.

III

Our leader arrives waving bogus passports
he's had forged by a certain printer, crazily
insisting their magic, rubbed off us, permits

passage to his new complete Democracy
of Love on earth. Utopias can be perfect
in the mind's nowheres, not in Wales, Italy

or here, yet I'm in love (and therefore suspect)
with the still unborn pure idea of him.
Isn't it the reality we reject

that shows we're sane? I watch stream from his head sperm,
all the children who'll outlive him. I too take
delight in magic ink, I too want freedom

to always begin, but when I kiss his cheek
the spell breaks. Practice makes imperfect. Flesh is weak.

IV

For six months the felons of Barnstaple
treated me to a quip about the last rung
of an Irish ladder. To be in gaol

for posting Mad Shelley's tracts was one thing,
I made the joke as his Irish footman.
But my mates and his critics couldn't wing

us quite. Then, before the panopticon
and moral profit, a soul could escape.
My riposte was to tell them that sign on

the last rung was an English plot to keep
us from upward flight. Reader, do you miss
Dan from the books? Do you guess I was dropped

for booze or women? Say I took off. Just
because you lose me doesn't mean I'm lost.

V
He's in the backseat of a gondola
chatting up some eligible daughter
in terms perhaps designed to kindle her

with notions and emotions he's taught her.
He sighs: 'O join me in my carmagnole!'
and they all collapse in girlish laughter

as the orchestra strikes up a barcarole,
for it's a movie and they act themselves.
In close-up he ad-libs some rigmarole

about Greece, oblivious to the waves
that flood the boat, weighed down in the canal
by a huge film crew. Byron wants to save

a few frames, but Shelley, who wants it all,
shouts: 'Show it speeded up, like *The General*!'

DAVID PARK

Lame Duck

Often one of them would be there when I
Came home from school, seated at a blazing
Fire with my mother, bright flames leaping high
Warming the whole room. To her they would bring
Their problems — my father called them mother's
Lame ducks — and with childish ignorance I
Hated their weakness and thought it unfair
That they had taken the place that was mine,
And so I skulked in a cold bedroom till
Each one had gone. Women were drawn to her,
The fragile branches of their lives heavy
With loneliness and shaken by despair.
There was one who could neither read nor write
And a woman who took turns and thought she
Was being followed. It always frightened
Me that she might decide to come and see
My mother when only I was there and
I would have to talk with her. In truth I
Despised them all and did not understand
Thinking life belonged to the high-fliers.

Years later I make my way through the dawn
Streets of Belfast with childish ideas stripped
Away. I struggle steadily on, drawn
Towards that warm hearth fire, my spirit clipped
And feathers coated with the thick black slime
Of disappointment. Old beliefs now ring
Hollow with the paring passage of time,
As I limp home with bruised and broken wings.

The Piano Miracle

Unplayed for twenty years,
Permanent pieces of furniture,
It sits barren as the fig tree
That both coercion and bribery
Have failed to remedy

Until tonight and this
Light-fingered stranger,
Who fills the house with
An exaltation of skylarks and
The low rumble of thunder.

We watch in wonder
At the miracle of the piano —
The alabaster box opened,
The withered hand healed,
A child born in old age.

Snow-drift

I have seen my mother weep three times,
The first as a child, when the bitter gall of grief
Blinded her eyes with burning tears
And breeched the reservoir of restraint,
And once among the ashes and blackened rubble
She turned her head away and shed furtive tears
For the battered and broken heart of a city.
Tonight she sits in a dusk-filled room
After the flickering television light has faded
And weeps silently for a lost humanity.

The fragile tears fall gently like snow-flakes,
I stand powerless to gather them.
They pile up in deep drifts about my heart.

The Fire at Crymble's Music Shop

Jimmy's Lament

It had an Edwardian Art Nouveau façade
Compact and neat like a tune on a pipe,
And weekly we would stage an admiring blockade
With periscopes up and landing party ready,
For though Constantinople might be the door
To the sultry East, Crymble's music shop
Was our passport to rock-'n'-roll's balmy shores.
With faces pressed against the window
Like hungry waifs at a bun-shop
We eye-feasted on the gleaming rows
Of instruments — finely varnished Spanish guitars
And spangling drum-kits with the skin
Glistening taut and white like
Polythene stretched over the top of a jam-jar.
But more than anything we coveted
Those bright red electric guitars,
Teenage icons, symbol of unbridled power,
Possessing chords that could split the atom
And crack the vaulted dome of Heaven.
Once outside the shop you declared
With mock declamation and profound insanity,
Life was an old rock-'n'-roll song no Greek tragedy.
We collapsed in laughter on the pavement.

'She wore a clingin' dress that fit so tight
She couldn't sit down so we danced all night.'

Bebop-a-lulu and good vibrations
With slicked back hair and evil leer,
Rubber legs and elasticated arms akimbo,
We practised Presley impersonations
Before the laughing mirror
The adult voice said Big Bopper Columbus
Had a lot to answer for
As Chick Berry duck-walked through 'Maybellene'

And Buddy Holly sang 'Rave On' on Mount Olympus.
Imported world of candy stores and junior proms,
If Peggy Sue won't go then Daisy May,
Paris wanted Helen to sing in his backing group,
Hamlet drove a metaphysical Chevrolet.
'Six hot-dogs oughta be just right
After such a wonderful night'
Shoobee-doobee-doo, multi-coloured hoola-hoops,
Is this the lyric that launched a thousand ships?

A plague on Sinatra's crooning, Little Richard's
Falsetto shivered the spine like an icicle.
Close one eye, Belfast Surf City,
We surfed on roller-skates
Cruised on second-hand bicycles.
We embraced the new wave of popular heroes,
Dylan, Lennon, Jagger,
And if the casualty rate rose a little higher
As Joplin, Jones and Hendrix departed from us,
The nagging post-mortems seemed superfluous —
In the end all energy consumes itself.

But now all has changed, and though the fire
That destroyed Crymble's was a single voice
In a massed choir of wanton destruction,
In some worlds it marked the end of an era
As we drown in a plethora of pastiche,
The gaucheness of nouveau sophistication.

Legato, Fortissimo, Pianissimo,
Mene mene tinkle ukulele
The writing was always on the wall.
The gutting flames play their own lament
As an elegy sounds on crackling chimes,
A wide-eyed dream fading into yesterday
Our youth burning in *adagio* time.

Beautiful Lofty Things

Beautiful lofty things: Denis Law's noble head;
Ken Clelland on a table, before him the graduates newly-fledged,
'An impressive sight', and as their cheers began to fade
'Plumeless peacocks arrayed in degrees of stupidity',
Laughter and beer in his beard, proposing a toast to Walter Mitty;
Crazy Charlie on a bicycle zig-zagging down Kilbride Street
Pursued by two breathless peelers with heavy sparking feet;
Andy Clarke leading out Mackie's strike for decent pay
Shaking a sledge-hammer fist at the bosses on the way;
Betty Williams leading the women up the Falls through
The rabid mob, abuse and stones falling like rain:
All the Olympians; a thing never known again.

Boys' Game

Sometimes seen, sometimes merely suspected
A grey slither, a startled warning shout
They threw stones at bushes, bravado bright
Frightened at what might suddenly leap out.

The boys are men now, though mostly in name.
Sitting on bar-stools cupping courage tight,
Sipping slow strength, the game remains the same
Only the targets changed by laughing time.

Throwing at God, the church, the bitching wife
Talking of giving it all up, new starts,
Cursing the treadmill job which blights their life
Composing speeches to denounce the boss.

Tossing stones, only pausing long enough
To pay their round, letting fire new surges
Of ardour, throwing all the harder, safe
In the knowledge that nothing will emerge.

Threading the Stars

The search for images is invariably graven
The hunting of symbols hopelessly askew —
There is no face behind the gimcrack mask.
The mounted metaphors of madness
Distort the simplicity of the chosen task,
Let the mind discard its devious schemes
And move through open paths to strike
The rock and free the flowing streams.

The battered bus speeds through the night
Along the back roads of Europe,
From the companion stranger
Comes a constant clicking noise
Like a broken tap dripping drops of water.
Sudden head-lights of a passing car
Fleet a glimpse of rosary beads and a pale face
Mouthing the dark night spaces, threading the stars.

Walking Over The Troubles

In my absence the carpet has been laid.
I come down in the morning to find it
Protected from the incursive sun by
Old newspapers, gilded with lists of dead,

Public pictures of other people's pain.
Headlines scream up raw as an open wound
But the names bring but a vague remembrance,
The seed of sorrow sown on stony ground.

Yesterday's land lies over distant seas
Behind high walls in self's safe world I live,
What I cannot touch hear or see soon grows
Callously cold. May they and God forgive

Me as with a heart harder than Pharaoh's
I pause, then walk over, terror's roll-call
Soon forgotten, water under the bridge,
Suffering under an indifferent soul.

My Grandfather

He sits bolt upright on the chair
Yesterday's paper on his knee
His eyes locked in an empty stare.

His mind is gone my mother says
But where it goes she does not know,
Perhaps gone back to long-lost days.

Gone to the summer fields of France
To count Ulster's myriad dead
When Haig gave orders to advance,

Gone down to the ship-yard to work
On the *Titanic,* mindless of
What dangers in deep waters lurk,

Gone to the allotment once more
Where with clay-caked fingers he grew
Flowers that scented the earth's core.

His mind has gone but I know where,
Gone to the dark woods, tracking the
Bright-eyed fox to its secret lair.

Pat Jennings

Tall as the Empire State and Broadway broad
He guards his goal with an agility
That leaves us standing open-mouthed like fish.
Once Swift ruled; but as he swallow-dives through
The air, reflexes sharp as winter front,
The crowd's acclaiming roar crowns a new king.
Once in a film I saw John Wayne dive in
Front of wild horses, but it pales to nothing
As, his own stunt man, he flings himself
Head-first at MacDonald's thundering hooves.
For lesser mortals the ball slips like soap
But he stands a pole apart from all these,
He scoops it up, his arm a trawler's net,
The ball an iron filing, each hand a magnet.

The Things that Frighten

The things that frighten any child are more
Real than doubt, surer than the shadow on
The nursery wall, a tightly shut door
That only time and patience may open.
Fear of the clutching dark, thunder's angry
Admonition, the empty house rustling
With silence like light footsteps on dead leaves;
Like thought-winged birds of prey they come swooping
In a taloned labyrinth of fierce beaks.
Was it just the rain stippling the window
Or pleading tears from some abandoned child,
Lost in loneliness, locked-out long ago?
Did we dare admit him? Would he bring the
Rich gift of love — gold, frankincense and myrrh —
Or some enticing evil that would spring
And trap us fast in an evil snare?
Thus with a curse they start up suddenly,
Flapping their black wings like hideous crows.
But passing years bring relief and in time
Most children cast them off like out-grown clothes.

The things that frighten any adult are
More strange and terrible still. Passing years
May exorcise impalpable spectres
And outlandish ghouls; subdue full-blown fears,
But others come to take their place, darting
Like dark swallows to vanish without trace
In a shiver, a shadow, the rippling
Of water by the wind before it calms
Over once more. And though sceptics we place
Our hand in the side of our risen fear,
Feel the nail-prints of our credulity,
In the end nothing is ever made clear.
Taking refuge in well-worn words we may
Dismiss them with a shrug, but no soothing
Incantations of reason can allay
Feelings of seeing through a glass darkly.

For say now why these should have frightened so —
An old man walking in the summer park,
Empty streets, a face glimpsed at a window,
The night birds coming slowly home to roost.

At the Vincent Van Gogh Museum

The museum is overrun by a flotilla
Of manoeuvring Americans. Girded in Instamatics
And posing as anointed art critics
They throw up a heavy flak in rust-red voices.
Most popular choice of citadels, the air is battered
With competitive sensitivity, splashed by the unholy water
Of benign condescension. Safely caged and contained,
He satisfies our romantic conception of the artist,
Extra joy, voyeur's reward, it is the spice we love the best,
Rejection, the dark web of madness, and that business
Of cutting off his ear and sending it to a whore.
Really nothing ever changes, we paid our money at the door
But would avoid a strange vision, terrible and unique,
Bring in the Gorgons, hunchbacks, and two-headed beasts
For in truth, we came to see a freak.

He stares down from a self-portrait, encased in timeless
Dignity, the dappled strokes rotating an ivory silence,
His scallop-shell eyes cold with death, warm with life.

The paintings wreak their own perpetual retribution,
A razor-mirror ruthlessly slicing through self-deception,
Prising open the shell, unspinning the consoling cocoon of pretension.
In the polished glass we see the reflection of our inadequacy.
Impennate creatures, the sky is out of reach, and so we
Grub in the dirt of experience to kindle a few sparks,
Counterfeit incandescence, they flicker in the conspiring dark
Then expire, leaving only the blackened ashes of bitterness.
The die is cast, content to journey with all the rest
We stumble along the broad road that leads to imperfection.
Despise us if you will, but stare down in quickening silence,
Let the sleeping sleep happily on the edge of the abyss.
Forgive us if you can, as peddling a maudlin merchandise
We bed down with the withered hag of self-satisfaction,
Suck the teat of mediocrity.

The Stained Shroud

Anoint the gaudy, the vulgar, and the cheaply brash,
Exalt high the low and cast down the high
(The Mona Lisa on the subway wall has a moustache).
At Westminster Abbey the sign says ice-cream is prohibited,
They welcome pilgrims, sinners and tourists, the merely
Curious, but draw the line at dripping cornets.
In Piccadilly Circus the capital's stinking armpit
The crowds queue four deep to see *The Happy Hooker*
And 'Do the Hustle' is number one in all the charts.
In the square outside Notre Dame a jazz band
Plays 'Yes Sir that's my Baby', and a blasé monkey
Passes round a hat for a performing man.
So come, dispatch your pathetic sense of aesthetics
And stuff your snobbish superiority, join the line to
Have your snapshot taken in the ovens at Auschwitz.
Art is a eunuch, sensitivity is a whore,
'Vulgarity, my dear, is all the rage',
God is a clown twice nightly on a West End stage.

Anne Frank's House

It is the simple things which sear the most —
Pencil marks showing the heights of growing
Children, the tiny pins which mark the just
Too slow advance and end so cruelly near,
The pictures she cut out of magazines
And pasted on the wall — all still here to
Chronicle a foreign world of formal
Intimacy and unremitting view
Where any accidental noise echoed
Eternally in a bell-jar of fear,
Splintering and disfiguring the mind's
Dreaming reflections, and where for two years
They hid embryo in the secret womb
Of the annex, starting at light and sound,
Knowing that it might soon become a tomb
Of aborted hope and stillborn desires.
The end came suddenly in a crash of
Footsteps on wooden stairs, soon after it,
The slow rumble of the last convoy of
Crowded cattle trucks heading for Auschwitz.

Suddenly our respectful silence is
Shattered by great gasping sobs, an old man
Is weeping in a corner of the room.
Among us all perhaps he understands
Too well, a black raven flapping across
His mind in a flurry of wire and lime,
A memory tattooed in blue ink which
Hangs from the meat-hooks of an evil time.
Perhaps the memory of something done
Or the doubly cold and bitter recall
Of the deed he left undone. Whatever,
This old man weeping unsettles us all.
In turn we turn our heads away and file
Out into the hot streets of the city,
Accusing thoughts soon stilled, a stranger's grief
Someone else's responsibility.

The Climber in the Cherry Blossom Tree

The great dark-veined, thin-fingered hand of waving pink
Conjures a magical host of blossom doves from its open palm
And sends them fluttering in drunken freedom across the laughing sky.
On an evening of blue-glass when only the rippling tree disturbs the calm
I lie on my back in the grass and watch her climb cat-like in its branches,
The tightness of her grip and the lightness of her fleet-footed step
Allowing her to walk on the bough's foaming waves without sinking,
And wrestle with fate that threatens to drown her in an ocean of pink.
She stops, and like a sailor in the crow's-nest gazes earnestly out to sea,
Phoebe, dragon-fly sister, what can you see from the cherry blossom tree?
'I can see China with its Great Wall and Square of Heavenly Peace
I will climb higher till I see the whole world curling like an answer
    below my feet.'
So up she climbs still higher, scurrying down a ceaseless flurry of blossom.
The ice-cool petals float down slowly like some long-forgotten dream,
Slowly down they fall, one following the other in an endless stream.
One lands inside my head, a ladder of pink blossom ascends into Heaven.

Teaching Billy to Read

The words are evil; grotesque gargoyles,
Hateful Hydras wreathed in fear,
They rear up black as slag heaps
Sheer as Everest, no place for the
Flailing tongue to find a hold.
The words are evil; slippery like eels
Invidious, insidious, mocking
Serpents slithering across the page.
Finger probing like a blind man's stick
Stumbling, fumbling, staggering
With weighted feet up the hill
He pauses on a remembered oasis.
'The sun is out John is happy.'
Off again, drowning, straw-clutching,
Eyes wide as the universe.
The words are evil; mysterious,
Spitefully secretive, inexplicably cruel.

Lost in the labyrinth
We go on trying to unlock the gate,
Catching swallows in buckets,
Measuring infinity inch by inch.

Violence

At first he stalks me stealthily like a hunter
Then grows bolder, pulling patience taut,
The persistent offender, pushing, goading.

A bad day. A sudden snap,
Frustration bursting like a red balloon
He receives the expected retribution.

The terrible collective intake of breath
Sounds the bestowing of their perverse respect.
Silence trembles like a cold-night star

We retreat to the back of our cages,
Nurse our wounds,
Hate each other through the bars.

Some of Robert Johnstone's poems have been published in *Fortnight, Honest Ulsterman, New Poetry, Poetry Review*, and in his pamphlet, *Our Lives are Swiss* (Ulsterman Publications); they have also been broadcast on BBC Radio 3.